Schochler Primary School
_____of_____

# HORSES SET II

# AMERICAN PAINT HORSES

Kristin Van Cleaf
ABDO Publishing Company

## visit us at
## www.abdopub.com

Published by ABDO Publishing Company, 4940 Viking Drive, Edina, Minnesota 55435.
Copyright © 2006 by Abdo Consulting Group, Inc. International copyrights reserved in all
countries. No part of this book may be reproduced in any form without written permission from
the publisher. The Checkerboard Library™ is a trademark and logo of ABDO Publishing
Company.

Printed in the United States.

Cover Photo: Corbis
Interior Photos: Corbis pp. 9, 12, 16, 17, 21; Peter Arnold p. 7; Ron Kimball pp. 5, 10, 11, 15;
    Visuals Unlimited p. 19

Series Coordinator: Heidi M. Dahmes
Editors: Heidi M. Dahmes, Stephanie Hedlund
Art Direction: Neil Klinepier

### Library of Congress Cataloging-in-Publication Data

Van Cleaf, Kristin, 1976-
    American paint horses / Kristin Van Cleaf.
        p. cm. -- (Horses. Set II)
    Includes bibliographical references and index.
    ISBN 1-59679-313-9
        1. American paint horse--Juvenile literature. I. Title.

SF293.A47V36 2005
636.1'3--dc22

2005042129

# CONTENTS

# WHERE AMERICAN PAINT HORSES CAME FROM

Horses are strong and beautiful animals. They descend from a small animal called eohippus that lived more than 55 million years ago. But, horses have changed much since then.

Humans and horses have been companions for hundreds of years. Before cars and trains, horseback was the fastest way to travel on land. Horses have helped people farm, settle land, deliver mail, and fight in wars.

Spaniards brought horses to North America in the 1500s. Before that time, most Native Americans had never seen these animals. However, horses soon became an important part of native life.

**Horses are built for running and working. On average, horses live to be between 20 and 25 years old.**

American paint horses were especially treasured. This is still true today. Many people enjoy riding, racing, and working with these specially colored horses.

# What Paint Horses Look Like

American paint horses are known for their colorful coat patterns. These beautiful horses come in a variety of patterns and colors. They have strong bones and are well-balanced. Their heads and necks display grace and elegance.

The American paint horse has a body that is perfect for ranch work. A paint horse's hindquarters are made of strong muscles. They have broad chests and a stock-horse body type.

Horses are measured in four-inch (10-cm) units called hands. This measurement is taken from the top of the **withers** to the ground. An average paint horse stands 14.2 to 16 hands high.

The American Paint Horse Association (APHA) was created to preserve and promote the paint horse. The APHA is the second-largest **breed** registry in the United States. It has strict guidelines that each horse must meet in order to be registered as an American paint horse.

People often confuse paint horses with pinto horses. The main difference between the two is that pintos are not a breed. They are classified by color.

# What Makes Paint Horses Special

American paint horses descended from horses brought to North America by Spaniards. Many of these animals escaped and formed herds of wild horses. They roamed the prairies and deserts of the western United States.

In the 1600s, horses were an important part of Native American life. The paint horse's beautiful coat made them especially prized. Some Native Americans believed paint horses had magical powers.

Cowboys tamed paint horses. They found that this **breed** works well with cattle. So, it became a strong, dependable ranch horse.

Over time, **breeding** has improved the athletic ability of paint horses. They are sturdy, intelligent, and willing animals. Paint horses are good for both ranch work and pleasure riding. They are also **rodeo** horses and show horses. They are even friendly with children.

*Native Americans used horses to hunt and to fight wars.*

# CARE

Giving an American paint horse proper care prevents many health problems. An owner is responsible for providing his or her animal with a dry home in a stable or a barn.

A paint horse's stall should be clean and have plenty of fresh air. Give your paint horse comfortable bedding to lie

upon. Bedding can be wood shavings, straw, or shredded hemp spread over the floor.

Grooming helps keep a paint horse healthy and its coat looking nice. Brushing removes dirt from the coat. A stabled horse should be groomed daily with a currycomb, a body brush, and a mane and tail comb.

Check your horse's feet daily. Use a hoof pick to remove dirt and stones from the feet. The hooves will need trimming every four to six weeks.

Check that the horseshoes are in good shape. A running or working paint horse needs horseshoes to protect its feet. Horseshoes that weigh about eight ounces (230 g) are common. Winter horseshoes have cleats to help keep the horse from slipping on ice or snow.

A paint horse should see a veterinarian at least once a year. Your horse's teeth may need to be **floated**. It should also receive shots against diseases.

**Opposite page: *Your horse should be able to lie down and turn around easily while inside its stall.***

# FEEDING

An American paint horse will drink about ten gallons (38 L) of water in a day. Make sure it has fresh, clean water. The horse can drink from a watering **trough**, a bucket, or even a fountain in the stall.

A paint horse eats grass, hay, and grain. Hay should be bundled up into a net or rack. Keep the hay dry, or it may become moldy and make the horse sick.

Grain provides a working paint horse with more energy than just grass and hay. Oats, corn, and barley are often mixed to make horse grain. The horse usually eats grain from a bucket or a feed trough.

Vitamins and other **supplements** can also be important for a horse's health. Salt is important because a horse loses salt when it sweats. A paint horse usually licks a block of salt to get this supplement.

Paint horses also like treats such as carrots, apples, and sugar cubes. But, these should only be given occasionally. Horses need healthy food, just like humans!

**Horses need to eat at least three times a day.**

# THINGS PAINT HORSES NEED

An American paint horse's equipment is called tack. Tack should fit well and be kept clean. This way, it will not irritate the horse or cause other problems.

Saddles come in two types. A western saddle has

*Many horse owners have a tack room. This is important for keeping their tack dry and secure.*

wide **stirrups** and a **horn**. It is best for working horses. An English saddle is flatter and lighter than a western saddle. It is used in racing, hunting, and fence jumping.

A saddle is set on top of a saddle pad. The pad absorbs sweat from the horse's back. It also protects the horse's back and sides from the rubbing of the saddle.

A bridle is used to control a paint horse. It is made of leather straps that fit over the horse's head. Reins and a bit attach to the straps. The bit is a piece of metal that fits in the horse's mouth.

Spurs and whips are used to give the horse signals. But, these items should only be used by a trained rider.

*Boots will keep your feet from slipping out of the stirrups.*

# How Paint Horses Grow

A baby American paint horse is called a foal. Paint horses are mammals, which means their foals are born live. Having one foal at a time is most common. The mother is usually **pregnant** for about 11 months.

Within an hour of being born, a foal will stand for the first time. It may wobble on its long, skinny legs. Its mother will help it to start drinking her milk.

By instinct, a foal will follow its mother. A foal can trot and gallop within 24 hours. However it will tire easily, so it needs a lot of rest.

A foal drinks its mother's milk and eats grass for about two months. After this time, it may start to share its mother's feed. When the foal is four and a half to six months old, it is **weaned** from its mother.

*Two paint horses do not always have a colored foal. So, painted foals are valuable.*

# TRAINING

Training begins soon after a foal's birth. The young foal will slowly become accustomed to people. As it grows, it will learn to wear a **halter**. After one year, it can be trained to wear a saddle.

Horses are creatures of habit. They learn every time they are ridden. When training, the teacher always uses the same words in the same tone of voice.

A trainer teaches a horse through conditioning. For example, a trainer sitting on a horse might squeeze his or her legs. The trainer continues this action until the horse gives the desired response.

The horse learns how to move from these signals. When a horse has learned to follow signals, it can learn more complicated activities. For example, a horse might learn to run when a racetrack gate swings open.

Paint horses are trained for many purposes. They work on ranches, or as trail mounts. No matter what its training, this amazing **breed** is still a favorite of many people throughout the world.

*Paint horses aren't the only horses that need halters. Halters are used to tie a horse up, lead a horse, or keep a horse from wandering away.*

# GLOSSARY

**breed** - a group of animals sharing the same appearance and characteristics. A breeder is a person who raises animals. Raising animals is often called breeding them.

**float** - to file down a horse's teeth in order to remove sharp edges.

**halter** - a rope or strap for leading or restraining an animal.

**horn** - a projection from a saddle that is used for tying a rope around.

**pregnant** - having one or more babies growing within the body.

**rodeo** - a show featuring cattle roping, bronco riding, or steer wrestling.

**stirrup** - one of a pair of loops or rings hanging from a saddle used as footholds to help in mounting and while riding.

**supplement** - something that improves or completes something else.

**trough** - a long, shallow container for the drinking water or feed of domestic animals.

**wean** - to accustom an animal to eat food other than its mother's milk.

**withers** - the highest part of a horse's back.

# WEB SITES

To learn more about American paint horses, visit ABDO Publishing Company on the World Wide Web at **www.abdopub.com**. Web sites about these horses are featured on our Book Links page. These links are routinely monitored and updated to provide the most current information available.

# INDEX